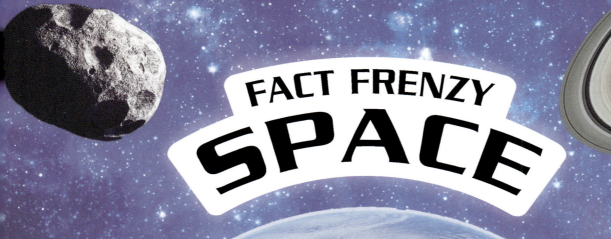

OUR SOLAR SYSTEM

Lisa Regan

Published in 2021 by
The Rosen Publishing Group, Inc.
29 East 21st Street, New York, NY 10010

Cataloging-in-Publication Data

Names: Regan, Lisa.
Title: Our solar system / Lisa Regan.
Description: New York : PowerKids Press, 2021. | Series: Fact frenzy: space | Includes glossary and index.
Identifiers: ISBN 9781725320246 (pbk.) | ISBN 9781725320260 (library bound) | ISBN 9781725320253 (6 pack)
Subjects: LCSH: Solar system--Juvenile literature.
Classification: LCC QB501.3 R465 2021 | DDC 523.2--dc23

Copyright © Arcturus Holdings Ltd, 2021

All rights reserved. No part of this book may be reproduced in any form without permission in writing from the publisher, except by a reviewer.

Manufactured in the United States of America

CPSIA Compliance Information: Batch CSPK20: For Further Information contact Rosen Publishing, New York, New York at 1-800-237-9932.

Contents

You live inside the sun
page 6

and other facts about the sun's atmosphere

You are always moving at super speed page 8

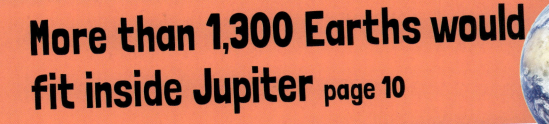

and other facts about Earth's orbit

More than 1,300 Earths would fit inside Jupiter page 10

and other facts about the planets

Our hottest planet isn't closest to the sun page 12

and other facts about Venus and Mercury

Pluto is only half as wide as the U.S. page 14

and other facts about Pluto

The moon may have been part of Earth page 16

and other facts about the moon

Earth has a second (mini) moon page 18

and other facts about other moons

Jupiter protects us from deadly comets page 20

and other facts about Jupiter

Our solar system is middle aged page 22

and other facts about the solar system

Life may be possible on other planets' moons page 24

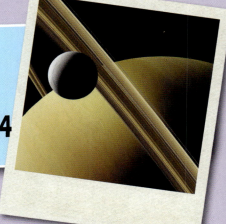

and other facts about life-forms on moons

Even More Facts! page 26

Glossary page 28

Further Information page 31

Index page 32

FACT 1 — YOU LIVE INSIDE THE SUN!

Earth is inside the sun's atmosphere, the layer of gases that surround the burning star. In fact, the whole of our solar system sits within the sun's atmosphere.

WARNING! LOOKING AT THE SUN, EVEN FOR A SECOND, CAN SERIOUSLY AND PERMANENTLY DAMAGE YOUR EYESIGHT. DON'T DO IT!

Layers of atmosphere

The sun's atmosphere is made up of three layers. The layer closest to the sun's surface is the photosphere, and it's so bright that usually it's the only part of the sun we can see. Next comes the chromosphere. The gases in this layer get hotter and hotter as they move out, reaching around 17,500°F (9,700°C). But that's nothing compared to the outer layer, the corona …

FACT 2 — The sun makes up more than 99% of the mass of the solar system. Jupiter makes up most of the rest.

The mighty corona

The corona is around 200 to 500 times hotter than the chromosphere layer below it, reaching up to 5.4 million °F (3 million °C). The corona stretches around 3 million miles (5 million km) into space, and then turns into the solar wind, the sun's flowing atmosphere that stretches across the solar system. Earth is within the reach of this solar wind, but luckily it cools down a lot before it gets to us!

Magnetic power

The corona's extreme heat might be linked to the fact that the sun is powerfully magnetic. Electric currents within the sun create a magnetic field that affects our entire solar system. One of the things this field does is protect us from 90% of the deadly cosmic rays moving through space. The amount of radiation that makes it through to Earth is low enough not to cause us problems.

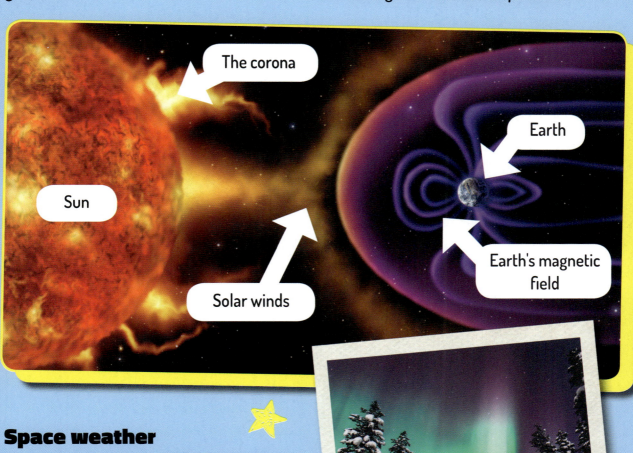

The corona
Sun
Solar winds
Earth
Earth's magnetic field

Space weather

Changes in the sun's magnetic field, such as powerful magnetic storms, can affect us on Earth. The sun shoots out solar winds, streams of speeding energy particles that can overcome Earth's own magnetic field and make our electronic objects stop working properly.

The Northern and Southern Lights occur when solar winds hit Earth's atmosphere.

7

FACT 3: YOU ARE ALWAYS MOVING AT SUPER SPEED

Even when you're just sitting on the couch watching TV, you're actually moving very fast! Earth travels 600 million miles (970 million km) around the sun each year.

Tied to the Sun

The sun is much bigger than Earth, so it has much stronger gravity. The sun pulls on Earth, so rather than Earth free-floating through space, it is tied to the sun and constantly travels around it in a set path.

This is called Earth's orbit around the sun, and it is more of a stretched egg shape than a perfect circle. The other planets in the solar system are also trapped, orbiting around the sun.

AROUND 1,300,000 EARTHS COULD FIT INSIDE THE SUN.

Good night, sun! We'll spin around and see you again tomorrow.

Spinning around

At the same time as Earth is moving around the sun, it is also constantly spinning around. From here on Earth, it looks like the sun is moving up and down and across the sky through the day. It's like when you look out of the window on a fast train and everything outside seems to be speeding past, but actually it is the train that is moving rather than anything outside.

FACT 4 If a human ran as fast as Earth moves around the sun, they'd finish seven back-to-back marathons in a single second!

Star safari

As Earth orbits the sun, it travels through different areas of space and we can see different stars. Earth always moves in the same direction around the sun and at roughly the same speed, so we know which stars and other objects in space we will be able to see at certain times of the year.

Chain of orbits

The sun does not stay still while Earth and the other planets in our solar system move around it. It orbits the middle point of our galaxy, the Milky Way, at around 143 miles (230 km) a second. The Milky Way orbits around a point between itself and the largest nearby galaxy, Andromeda. And our entire Local Group of galaxies orbits within a larger group, called the Virgo Supercluster, which itself moves around other bigger structures. It's exhausting!

FACT 5
MORE THAN 1,300 EARTHS WOULD FIT INSIDE JUPITER

The moon is a long way from Earth, around 238,900 miles (384,400 km). If you lined up all the planets in our solar system end to end, they could fit in the space between Earth and the moon.

The little ones

The four inner planets in the solar system—Mercury, Venus, Earth, and Mars—don't take up very much space at all. Mercury is the smallest planet, and could fit inside Earth 18 times over. Scientists think that some of Mercury's surface might have been burned off when it was forming, because of it being so close to the sun. Its huge, liquid, metal core makes up 75% of its total size, which is unusual for a planet.

"Jump in, Mercury, there's lots of room!"

The frozen giants

It's a big jump in size from the inner planets to the outer frozen giants. Jupiter and Saturn are gas giant planets, while Neptune and Uranus are ice giants. Neptune and Uranus are around four times the size of Earth, but Uranus is a little bigger than Neptune. Neptune is a bit heavier than Uranus, though, because of the different materials in its core.

The big players

The planet taking up the most space by far in this lineup would be Jupiter. It is so big that all the other planets in the solar system could fit inside it with plenty of room to spare. Saturn is the second-largest planet in our solar system and, like Jupiter, it is called a gas giant. Gas giants have a small, rocky core but are mostly made up of layers of liquid and gas.

Speeding through space

Despite the huge distance between Earth and the moon, it only takes about three days for a spacecraft to travel there! A spacecraft has to be going very fast to break away from Earth's gravity and out into space—around 7 miles (11 km) a second, which means a speedy journey to the moon. The moon is working against us, though ... it's moving 1.5 inches (3.8 cm) farther away from Earth each year!

FACT 6: OUR HOTTEST PLANET ISN'T CLOSEST TO THE SUN

Mercury may be the closest planet to the sun, but it's fiery Venus that takes the top hot spot in our solar system. The second planet from the sun is a meltingly hot 864°F (462°C).

Volatile Venus

Venus can often be seen with the naked eye from Earth. Looking at this beautiful, bright planet shining in the sky, you'd never know how brutal it is down on its surface. As well as being burning hot, it also has such thick clouds of acid that almost no sunlight gets through, making it a dark and gloomy place. Add in its raging winds, wild storms, volcanoes, and crushing air pressure, and it's not looking very appealing ...

I'm hot stuff!

FACT 7: Venus's hurricanes are over twice as fast as the strongest hurricanes on Earth.

Locking in heat

Venus's atmosphere, the layer of gases that surround planets, is mainly made of carbon dioxide. Venus is hot because of the "greenhouse effect" created by carbon dioxide, which traps a lot of the sun's heat and only lets a small amount of it back out into space again. This is also happening on Earth and causing global warming.

Rays   Heat

Moon-like Mercury

Over on Mercury (below), it's a bit calmer than on Venus. In fact, it looks very much like the moon! Mercury's surface is also rocky and covered with craters . Another similarity between Mercury and the moon is that they both have only a very, very thin atmosphere. As the closest planet, Mercury gets a lot of heat from the sun, but almost all of it quickly escapes back into space again.

Too hot and too cold!

It is still incredibly hot on Mercury at times, though. When it faces the sun, Mercury's surface can reach 801 °F (427 °C)—almost as hot as Venus. But when it spins away from the sun and night falls, the temperature can get as cold as -290 °F (-180 °C). The hottest and coldest temperatures ever recorded on Earth are 134 °F (56.7 °C) and -128.6 °F (-89.2 °C).

FACT 8: PLUTO IS ONLY HALF AS WIDE AS THE U.S.

Poor Pluto. It used to be considered the ninth planet in our solar system, but scientists have realized that it's just too small to be a real planet.

Days of glory

For 76 years, Pluto was part of an elite group—the planets of our solar system. First discovered in 1930, it was believed to be the most distant planet from the sun. But in 2006, scientists decided it isn't a planet after all. It meets the first two "musts" of being a planet—circling a star (the sun) and having enough gravity to pull itself into a round, 3-D shape—but fails the final test ...

THE LARGEST OF PLUTO'S FIVE MOONS, CHARON, IS SO BIG THAT IT MAKES PLUTO WOBBLE.

United States

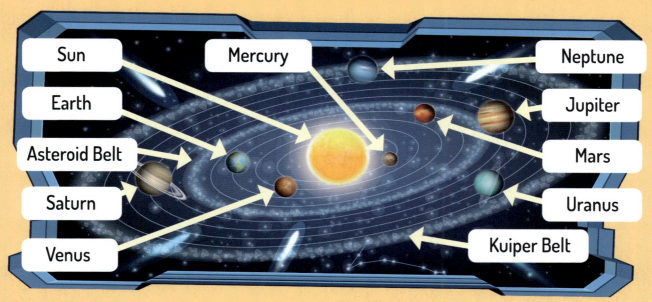

Sharing space

Pluto hasn't managed to clear the area around it of other objects, which is the third thing a planet needs to do. It is part of the Kuiper Belt, an area of icy objects on the outskirts of our solar system, and it still shares its space with a number of other large objects. It is too small to have strong enough gravity to either trap large nearby objects in its gravity or to throw them out into space.

Tough decisions

There was a lot of global debate between scientists before Pluto was downgraded from a planet to a dwarf planet. If scientists had allowed Pluto to be considered a planet despite only meeting two out of the three standards, other objects in our solar system—including many moons—would also have to be considered planets. We could have ended up with dozens of official planets—that's a lot of names to remember!

Dwarf planets

At the moment, Pluto is one of five official dwarf planets in our solar system. Three of the other dwarf planets—Haumea, Makemake, and Eris—are near Pluto, in the Kuiper Belt. Ceres is the only dwarf planet in the asteroid belt, between Mars and Jupiter. Scientists believe there are many more dwarf planets in our solar system that we haven't yet discovered—up to 200 in the Kuiper Belt and 10,000 in the area beyond.

FACT 9 — Several moons in our solar system are larger than the dwarf planets, but can't be dwarf planets because they orbit a planet themselves.

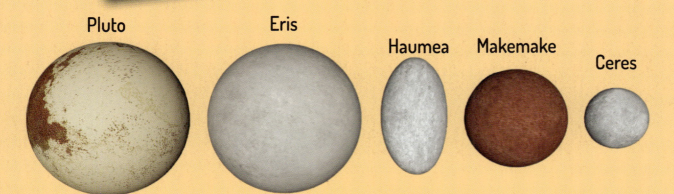

FACT 10: THE MOON MAY HAVE BEEN PART OF EARTH

Many scientists believe that the moon is made from material that chipped off of Earth when an object the size of Mars crashed into our young planet around 4.45 billion years ago.

Violent beginnings

That long ago, Earth would only have been around 50 million years old and the solar system would also only recently have come together. In these early stages, big crashes were very common. Many scientists think that the huge amounts of hot, rocky material blown off Earth by this crash got trapped by Earth's gravity and circled around Earth, eventually clumping together to create the moon.

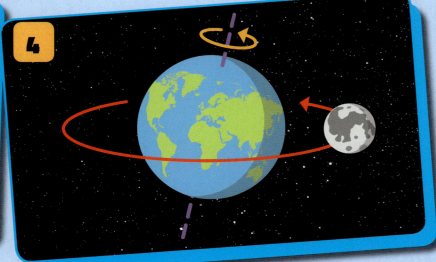

The Big Splash theory

This moon creation story is often called the "Big Splash" theory. It fits with some things we have learned about the moon. Astronauts have collected rock samples from the moon that are similar in some ways to rocks found on Earth. Also, the moon doesn't have much iron compared to Earth, but most of Earth's iron is in its core, so if the moon is made of its rocky outer layer this would make sense.

This moon rock was collected during the *Apollo 15* mission in 1971.

Other moon theories

It's important to remember that scientists do not always agree on a single theory, although often one idea becomes more popular than others over time. Some scientists still believe that the moon is one huge chunk chipped off of Earth, rather than lots of bits of material that later joined together. Others think that it was a large passing object that was trapped in Earth's gravity when it got too close.

Tilted Earth

Imagine grabbing a pole in a fire station and swinging around and around on it in one direction. Earth constantly spins like this around its axis, an imaginary pole running through its middle. Except its axis doesn't stand up exactly straight—it tilts a bit to one side. It is widely thought that this is because when the large object hit Earth and created the moon, the force of it also knocked Earth permanently off kilter.

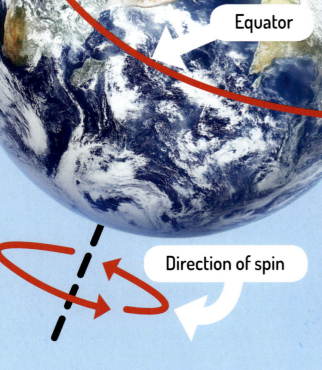

FACT 11: EARTH HAS A SECOND (MINI) MOON

The asteroid 2016 HO3 is circling Earth like the moon we all know and love, and has probably been doing so for the last 100 years.

"Get out! I'm the only real moon."

"Shhh, I just want a nice family picture."

EARTH'S MOON IS UNUSUALLY LARGE COMPARED TO OUR PLANET'S SIZE.

A sort-of moon

Asteroid 2016 HO3 is not exactly a true moon, as it drifts a little behind or ahead of Earth as it circles our planet. Another name for a moon is a natural satellite—it orbits a planet just like artificial weather and television satellites orbit Earth. Asteroid 2016 HO3 is a quasi-satellite—in other words, a sort-of moon—because it doesn't stick close enough to Earth.

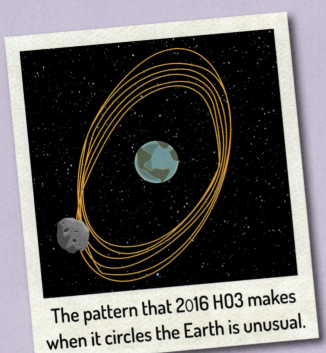

The pattern that 2016 HO3 makes when it circles the Earth is unusual.

Dancing with Earth

Although asteroid 2016 HO3 is around 100 times farther away from Earth than the moon, and doesn't stick as closely to us, it definitely has a long-term connection to Earth. It will be with us for centuries to come. Other asteroids sometimes get trapped in Earth's gravity and, as NASA puts it, "dance with Earth" for a while, but only for a short time and then they are back off on their way.

No-moon mystery

Neither Mercury nor Venus has a moon. Mercury doesn't have a moon because it is so close to the sun that its own gravity could never compete with the sun's pull. It is more of a mystery as to why Venus doesn't have a moon. Many scientists think it's still too close to the sun, some think its moon was destroyed, and others think that it "gave" Earth a moon. How generous!

FACT 12: Ganymede and Titan, Jupiter's and Saturn's largest moons, are both bigger than Mercury.

Many moons

Smaller planets tend to have few or no moons, whereas larger planets can have huge numbers of them. Scientists think that Jupiter has 79 known moons in total, the highest number in our solar system, although only 53 have been officially named so far. Twelve of the planet's moons were only discovered for the first time in 2017.

FACT 13 JUPITER PROTECTS US FROM DEADLY COMETS

Some scientists believe that one reason we are able to live on Earth is because Jupiter's strong gravity helps to pull fast-moving comets away from Earth and throw them back out of our solar system.

Giant protectors

With Jupiter's help, these really fast comets only hit Earth very rarely, every few millions or even tens of millions of years. Without Jupiter nearby, some scientists believe that comets would crash into Earth far more often. There are other scientists who think that Saturn also plays a big role in protecting Earth, and that it's only the combined force of Jupiter's and Saturn's gravity that is strong enough to make a difference.

COMETS ARE MADE OF ICE, DUST, AND ROCK, WHILE ASTEROIDS ARE USUALLY MADE OF METAL AND ROCK.

Leave my friend alone!

Thanks, Jupiter.

FACT 14 The first crash seen between two natural objects in space was Comet Shoemaker–Levy 9 hitting Jupiter in 1994.

Scars on Jupiter

Although Jupiter may play a role in protecting Earth from speeding comets, space objects such as comets and asteroids crash into Jupiter very often. When Comet Shoemaker-Levy 9 smashed into Jupiter, its pieces created dark scars on the planet's surface that were visible from Earth. In 2009, a dark spot the size of Earth was seen on Jupiter, believed to be damage caused by an asteroid only around 1,640 feet (500 m) wide.

Everyday scientists

Amateur astronomers—people who are not professional scientists but enjoy looking at and learning about space—have seen many objects crash into Jupiter in recent years. If seen in real time, this looks like a big "flash" of light, and the time it lasts tells us how large and heavy the object is. Amateurs' photos and videos are very useful, as professional telescopes don't always happen to be looking in the right place at the right time.

Asteroid crashes

While Jupiter often protects Earth from crashes, its strong gravity can sometimes work against us and send the occasional space object speeding in our direction instead—yikes! Some scientists believe Jupiter may have played a role in sending a huge asteroid to Earth 66 million years ago and killing off the dinosaurs, which let mammals grow and humans eventually evolve.

Dinosaurs may have been killed off by an asteroid crashing into Earth.

FACT 15: OUR SOLAR SYSTEM IS MIDDLE AGED

Our solar system is about halfway through its (very long) life. Scientists think our solar system began around 4.6 billion years ago and will survive for another 5 billion years

Wow, that's an old rock!

This meteorite fell to Earth near Buenos Aires, Argentina.

Radioactive dating

So how do scientists know how old the solar system is in the first place? They can find out the age of ancient rocks and meteorites by looking at how radioactive materials in them have broken down over time. Radioactive materials give out radiation and break down very predictably, so scientists can work backward from their current state to tell their age. The oldest meteorites from our solar system that have ever been dated are 4.56 billion years old.

Running out of fuel

The sun burns up its stores of hydrogen as fuel to survive. So far it has used about half of its hydrogen, so it has another 5 billion years' worth. Once it has burned up all this hydrogen, it will have to use its other materials for fuel, and then it will begin to die.

A giant sun

As the sun dies it will get much, much bigger and hotter, becoming a red giant star. It will grow out to reach Earth, perhaps farther, probably destroying our planet as well as Mercury and Venus. Some scientists believe that Earth might instead be pushed out into space rather than burned up by the sun. Either way, by this time Earth will be way too hot to support life.

Life after Earth

As the sun grows into a red giant, and planets and moons farther out in our solar system grow warmer, life may be possible there for a while. As the sun then shrinks and becomes a white dwarf, these planets will continue circling the sun's cold, dim remains for a long time. Scientists are searching for planets outside our solar system that may be able to support human life in the future.

23

FACT 16 LIFE MAY BE POSSIBLE ON OTHER PLANETS' MOONS

For a long time, scientists concentrated on finding other planets that may support alien life. Now, they are equally concerned about whether other planets could support humans.

Living on a moon

Jupiter and Saturn have lots of moons, and scientists believe that life may be able to evolve on some of them. We may think of our moon as a cold, empty place, but if humans need to leave Earth in the future, a moon might be our best option. With the help of advanced technology, we may be able to create an environment in which we can survive there.

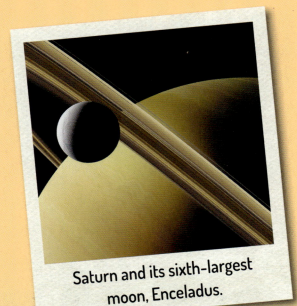

Saturn and its sixth-largest moon, Enceladus.

FACT 17 Jupiter's moons Io, Ganymede, Europa, and Calisto are so big you can see them with just a pair of binoculars.

We don't know what aliens might look like, but it's unlikely they'll be like in the movies!

Moon oceans

Saturn's moon Enceladus and Jupiter's moon Europa both have liquid water oceans under their frozen surfaces. Saturn's moon Titan has an ocean of liquid methane (a gas on Earth) rather than water. Although scientists don't think this methane ocean could support any life-forms familiar to us, it's possible that very different life-forms could evolve in space and survive in this kind of environment.

Alien life

Scientists are hopeful enough about the possibility of life-forms existing on Europa that a team once purposely destroyed a satellite heading toward Europa to stop it from crash-landing and possibly hurting alien life. The Cassini spacecraft has recently explored Enceladus and found conditions in its oceans similar to those that we believe led to early life on Earth.

THE SEARCH FOR EXTRATERRESTRIAL LIFE IS OFTEN SHORTENED TO "SETI."

Better off on Earth

As far as we know, Earth is the only planet that is perfectly suited for humans to live on—as long as we treat it with respect. We need to stop global warming so we aren't forced off Earth before we have the technology to survive elsewhere. Positive change is possible! We've already shrunk the hole in the ozone layer—a part of our atmosphere that protects us from the sun's heat—just by stopping using certain chemicals.

EVEN MORE FACTS!

You've found out lots about the solar system, but there's always more to discover! Boost your knowledge here with even more facts.

Galileo Galilei (1564-1642) was an Italian astronomer, physicist, and engineer. He developed a telescope that allowed the close observation of planets. He discovered, among other things, sunspots and Jupiter's four moons.

Sunspots are dark patches that appear on the sun's surface. They look dark because they are cooler than the rest of the sun. Some spots are wider than Earth. They increase and decrease in size regularly about every 10.8 years.

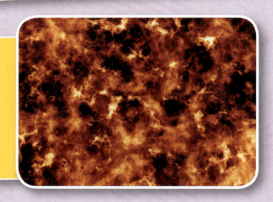

Isaac Newton (1643-1727) was an English scientist who developed the theory of gravity, the laws of motion, and a new type of math called calculus. His laws of dynamics and gravity helped explain the physics behind the solar system.

Every few months, the moon passes directly between the sun and Earth—a solar eclipse. The sun seems to turn black and it's possible to see its glowing corona around the edge of the moon.

A lunar eclipse happens when the moon passes behind Earth and into its shadow. During a total lunar eclipse, the moon looks brownish-red as it reflects light that is refracted by Earth's atmosphere.

Mercury is only slightly larger than our moon. As well as being the smallest planet in the solar system, it is also the fastest—orbiting the sun in just 88 Earth days.

Venus has mountains, valleys, and thousands of volcanoes. Its highest mountain, Maxwell Montes, is 36,000 feet (10,970 m) high, similar to Earth's highest mountain, Mount Everest.

The only spacecraft to visit Pluto is New Horizons, which passed close by in July 2015. The spacecraft provided the first close-up images of Pluto, showing ice plains, mountains, and heart-shaped glaciers.

We only ever see one side of the moon. This is because it rotates on its own axis at the same rate that it orbits around Earth. To see the other side, you would have to go into space.

Jupiter has such a strong gravitational field that you would weigh 2.5 times as much on Jupiter as you do on Earth.

SOLAR SYSTEM GLOSSARY

Apollo A space program consisting of manned U.S. spacecraft designed to explore the moon and surrounding space.

asteroid A small, rocky object made up of material left over from the birth of the solar system.

asteroid belt A region between the orbits of Mars and Jupiter, containing a concentration of asteroids moving around the sun.

astronomer A scientist who studies the stars, planets, and other natural objects in space.

atmosphere A shell of gases kept around a planet, star, or other object by its gravity.

axis An imaginary line through the middle of something.

chromosphere The middle layer of the sun's atmosphere, between the photosphere and the corona.

comet A chunk of rock and ice from the edge of the solar system.

corona The outer layer of the sun's atmosphere.

cosmic rays Radiation consisting of particles of very high energy that reach Earth from outer space.

crater A very large hole in the ground created by something hitting it or by an explosion.

dwarf planet A world, orbiting a star, that looks like a planet but does not meet certain criteria needed to make it a true planet.

eclipse An eclipse of the sun is when the moon is between Earth and the sun, so that for a short time you cannot see part or all of the sun. An eclipse of the moon is when Earth is between the sun and the moon, so that for a short time you cannot see part or all of the moon.

equator An imaginary line around the middle of Earth, at an equal distance from the North Pole and the South Pole.

galaxy A large system of stars, gas, and dust, with anything from millions to trillions of stars.

glacier An extremely large mass of ice that moves very slowly, often down a mountain valley.

global warming The gradual rise in Earth's temperature caused by high levels of carbon dioxide and other gases in the atmosphere.

gravity A natural force created around objects with mass, which draws other objects toward them.

greenhouse effect The problem caused by increasing quantities of gases such as carbon dioxide in the air, which trap the sun's heat and cause a gradual rise in the temperature of Earth's atmosphere.

hydrogen A colorless gas that is the lightest and most common element in the universe.

Kuiper Belt A ring of small, icy worlds directly beyond the orbit of Neptune. Pluto is the largest known Kuiper Belt object.

magnetic field The area around a magnet, or an object acting like a magnet, in which the magnetic power to attract is felt.

meteorite A large piece of rock or metal from space that has landed on Earth.

methane A colorless gas that has no smell.

Milky Way Our home galaxy, a spiral with a bar across its core. Our solar system is about 28,000 light-years from the monster black hole at its heart.

moon Earth's closest companion in space, a ball of rock that orbits Earth every 27.3 days. Most other planets in the solar system have moons of their own.

NASA An abbreviation for "National Aeronautics and Space Administration," the American government organization concerned with spacecraft and space travel.

orbit A fixed path taken by one object in space around another because of the effect of gravity.

ozone layer The part of Earth's atmosphere that has the most ozone in it. The ozone layer protects living things from the harmful radiation of the sun.

SOLAR SYSTEM GLOSSARY continued

photosphere The layer of the sun's atmosphere closest to its surface.

planet A world, orbiting a star, which has enough mass and gravity to pull itself into a ball-like shape, and clear space around it of other large objects.

radiation Very small particles of a radioactive substance.

radioactive Being capable of giving off energy in the form of particles or rays that can be powerful and harmful.

red giant A huge, very bright star near the end of its life, with a cool, red surface. Red giants are stars that have used up their fuel supply.

satellite Any object orbiting a planet. Moons are natural satellites made of rock and ice. Artificial satellites are machines in orbit around Earth.

solar system The eight planets (including Earth) and their moons, and other objects such as asteroids, that orbit around the sun.

solar wind The constant stream of charged particles sent out by the sun at high speeds. It interacts with Earth's magnetic field and causes aurorae, or flickering bands of light, also called the polar lights, northern lights, or southern lights.

spacecraft A vehicle that travels into space.

telescope A device that collects light or other radiations from space and uses them to create a bright, clear image. Telescopes can use either a lens or a mirror to collect light.

white dwarf The dense, burned-out core of a star like the sun, collapsed to the size of the Earth but still intensely hot.

FURTHER INFORMATION

BOOKS

Aguilar, David. *Space Encyclopedia.* London, UK: National Geographic Kids, 2013.

Becklade, Sue. *Wild About Space.* Thaxted, UK: Miles Kelly, 2020.

Betts, Bruce. *Astronomy for Kids: How to Explore Outer Space with Binoculars, a Telescope, or Just Your Eyes!* Emeryville, CA: Rockridge Press, 2018.

DK. *The Astronomy Book: Big Ideas Simply Explained.* London, UK: DK, 2017.

DK. *Knowledge Encyclopedia Space!: The Universe as You've Never Seen it Before.* London, UK: DK, 2015.

Frith, Alex, Jerome Martin, and Alice James. *100 Things to Know About Space.* London, UK: Usborne Publishing, 2016.

National Geographic Kids. *Everything: Space.* London, UK: Collins, 2018.

WEBSITES

Ducksters Astronomy for Kids
http://www.ducksters.com/science/astronomy.php
Head to this website to find out all there is to know about astronomy. You can also try an astronomy crossword puzzle and word search!

NASA Science: Space Place
https://spaceplace.nasa.gov
Discover all sorts of facts about space, other planets, and the moon. You can even play the Mars Rover Game, sending commands to the Mars rover and collecting as much data as possible in eight expeditions!

Science Kids: Space for Kids
http://www.sciencekids.co.nz/space.html
Go beyond our planet and explore space through fun facts, games, videos, quizzes and projects.

Publisher's note to educators and parents: Our editors have carefully reviewed these websites to ensure that they are suitable for students. Many websites change frequently, however, and we cannot guarantee that a site's future contents will continue to meet our high standards of quality and educational value. Be advised that students should be closely supervised whenever they access the Internet.

INDEX

A
aliens 24–25
Andromeda 9
Apollo 15 17
asteroid 2016 HO3 18–19
asteroid belt 15
asteroids 18–19, 20, 21
astronauts 17
astronomers 21, 26
atmosphere 6, 7, 13, 25
axis 17

B
Big Splash theory 17

C
carbon dioxide 13
Cassini 25
Charon 14
chromosphere 6, 7
clouds 12
comets 20, 21
Comet Shoemaker-Levy 21
core 10, 11, 17
corona 6, 7
cosmic rays 7
crashes 16, 20, 21
craters 13

D
dinosaurs 21
dwarf planets 14, 15

E
eclipse 26
electronics 7
Equator 17

G
galaxies 9
Galileo 26
gases 6, 11, 13, 23, 25
global warming 13, 25
gravity 8, 11, 14, 16, 17, 19, 20, 21, 26
greenhouse effect 13

H
hydrogen 23

J
Jupiter 6, 11, 15, 19, 20–21, 24, 25, 27

K
Kuiper Belt 15

L
Local Group 9
lunar eclipse 26

M
magnetic fields 7
magnetic storms 7
Mars 10, 15
Mercury 10, 12, 13, 15, 19, 23, 27
meteorites 22
methane 25
Milky Way 9
moon (Earth's) 10, 11, 13, 16–17, 18, 19, 26, 27
moons 14, 15, 18–19, 24–25

N
Neptune 11, 15
Newton, Isaac, 26
Northern Lights 7

O
oceans 25
orbits 8–9, 23, 27
ozone layer 25

P
photosphere 6
planets 10–15, 23
Pluto 14–15, 27

R
radiation 7, 22
red giant stars 23

S
satellites 18, 19, 25
Saturn 11, 15, 19, 24, 25
solar eclipse 26
solar wind 7
Southern Lights 7
spacecraft 11, 25, 27
space travel 11, 25
speed 8, 9, 11
stars 9, 23
storms 12
sun 6–7, 8, 9, 15, 23
sunspots 26

T
temperatures 7, 12, 13, 23, 25

U
Uranus 11, 15

V
Venus 10, 12, 13, 15, 19, 23, 27
Virgo Supercluster 9
volcanoes 12, 27

W
white dwarf star 23
winds 12